THE BATMAN MOVIE

RISE OF THE ROGUES

by Beth Davies

Batman created by Bob Kane with Bill Finger

BANG!

Editor Pamela Afram
Designer Sam Bartlett
Senior Editor Hannah Dolan
Senior Designer Nathan Martin
Pre-production Producer Siu Yin Chan
Producer Louise Daly
Managing Editor Paula Regan
Design Managers Guy Harvey and Jo Connor
Publisher Julie Ferris
Art Director Lisa Lanzarini
Publishing Director Simon Beecroft

Batman created by Bob Kane with Bill Finger

First published in Great Britain in 2017 by Dorling Kindersley Limited
80 Strand, London WC2R 0RL
A Penguin Random House Company

10 9 8 7 6 5 4 3 2 1
001–297917–Jan/2017

A WORLD OF IDEAS:
SEE ALL THERE IS TO KNOW

www.dk.com
www.LEGO.com

Contents

Gotham City

Gotham City is a busy place, with lots of citizens.

Commissioner Jim Gordon is the Head of Police. It is his job to stop crime in the city.

Jim is soon going to retire from the job. His daughter, Barbara, is going to take over.

The Hero Team

Sometimes, Gotham City
needs heroes! When a mission
is too dangerous for the police
alone, the police commissioner
shines the Bat-Signal.
Batman sees its light shining
and rushes to the rescue.
Batman likes to work alone,
but sometimes he needs help.
Robin and Batgirl help
him to catch criminals
and save the day.
Three heroes are
better than one!

COMMISSIONER JIM GORDON

WANTS YOU TO HELP KEEP

GOTHAM CITY SAFE

Citizens of Gotham City, please alert the police if you see any of the following:

 A **cat-like** woman prowling around jewellery stores.

 A man holding a giant **question mark**. Do not approach him! Conversation may cause confusion.

 A red-haired woman surrounded by wriggling **plants**.

 A man with a huge, **toothy grin**. Do not be fooled by his friendly appearance!

 GOTHAM CITY POLICE DEPARTMENT

 I BELIEVE IN BATMAN

KEEPING
GOTHAM CITY
SAFE

Meet the Rogues

Gotham City's villains have started working together, too. Their team is known as the Rogues.

Each of these crooks has fought
Batman many times in the past.
He has beaten each one alone,
but never all of them at once!
Batman will have to use all of
his gadgets to save the day.

The Joker

The Joker is Batman's foe. He likes to cause trouble and create chaos in the city. The only thing that the Joker takes seriously is committing crime.

The Joker believes he is Batman's worst enemy. Batman does not agree. This wipes the smile off the Joker's face.

My <u>Worst</u> Enemy
by the Joker

Batman never laughs at my jokes, even though they are really funny!

He always tries to stop me from getting away from crime scenes.

He thinks he is really strong,
but I always have the last laugh!

Batman likes to take pictures
without me in them!

Harley Quinn

Harley Quinn is one
of the Joker's closest
allies. She loves his silly
pranks and nasty tricks.
Her colourful costume and
bright make-up are nearly
as eye-catching as the Joker's.
Harley used to be a doctor,
but now she causes chaos.
Batman should watch out
for her swinging bat.

The Joker's Notorious *Lowrider*

The car can bounce up and down

Silly golden chicken decoration

Joker

Wheels spinning at top speed

The Joker and Harley Quinn drive around Gotham City in the Joker's Notorious Lowrider. They create as much chaos as they can. This wacky vehicle looks harmless, but it is perfect for scaring people!

Music system hides button for missile launcher

Handles for Harley Quinn to grip on to while skating

A missile launcher is hidden inside the boot

Horn to make people jump

The Riddler

One of the most confusing criminals in Gotham City is the Riddler. He leaves tricky puzzles at crime scenes for Batman to solve.

If Batman follows the tyre tracks of the Riddler's Riddle Racer, he might be able to stop this Rogue once and for all. Or could this be another trick?

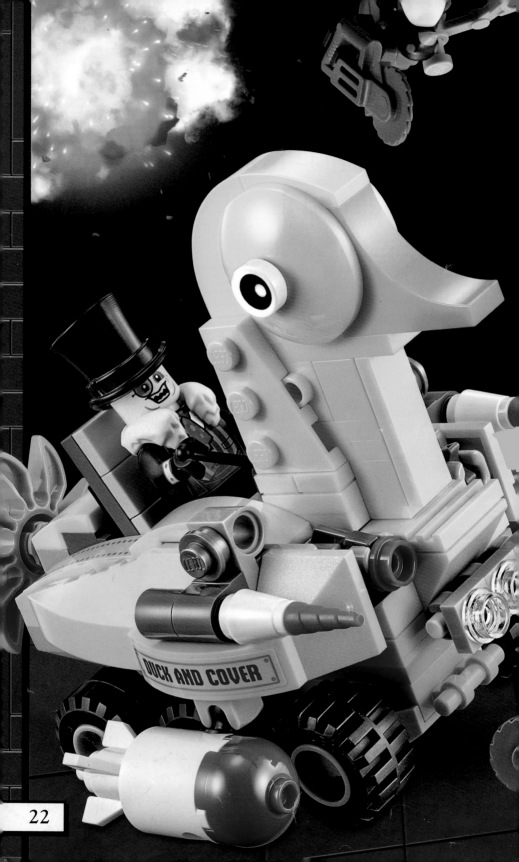

DUCK AND COVER

This businessman is no birdbrain!
The Penguin controls lots of gangs
in Gotham City. This has made
him very rich. He wears an
expensive top hat and suit.

The Penguin attacks Batman's
Batcave with an army of penguin
friends. His getaway vehicle is
shaped like a duck.

Mr. Freeze

This frosty villain sends a chill
down Batman's spine. He wears
a large, armoured suit that keeps
him ice-cold at all times.

Mr. Freeze is a scientist. He even
invented his own freeze gun.
He attacks the Gotham City
Energy Facility with the rest of the
Rogues. When he tells the scared
workers to "freeze", they really do!

Killer Croc

Killer Croc is one of Batman's most fearsome foes. He has a powerful tail, scaly skin and snapping teeth – just like a real crocodile!

Killer Croc's truck is perfect for driving through swamps. It has large wheels and a big headlamp. Killer Croc controls the vehicle from a section at the back. He is so big, he cannot fit in the driver's seat!

Catwoman

This crook is very good at breaking into buildings. Catwoman loves stealing from rich people in Gotham City. Her favourite things to steal are precious gems. This jewellery shop is a perfect target!

Catwoman makes a speedy getaway on her purple motorcycle. Luckily, Robin and Batgirl are right on her tail!

Poison Ivy

This Rogue likes plants much
more than humans. Even her
outfit is inspired by flowers. She has
green-fingered gloves, and she
wears leaves in her red hair.

Poison Ivy has special powers. She can control all forms of plant life. Poison Ivy wants to trap Batman in her tangling tendrils.

Clayface

Clayface is the biggest and messiest of Batman's foes. He is made of mud and can transform into different shapes. He creates giant mud fists for attacking his enemies.

Clayface loves to destroy everything around him. Batman must watch out for the splats of mud he fires to stick people to the ground.

The Joker's Plan

The Joker is very clever. He has come up with a cunning plan. He wants to destroy Gotham City Energy Facility, which supplies all the power to the city. Gotham City will be in total chaos and the Joker will take over!

THE JOKER'S FUNHOUSE

Hi, everyone. It's the Joker! I have created my very own funhouse in Gotham City. Come inside. You won't be able to stop smiling. But you MUST follow these rules...

DO:

- ☑ Bring rubber chickens

- ☑ Wear purple and green

- ☑ Laugh at all of my jokes

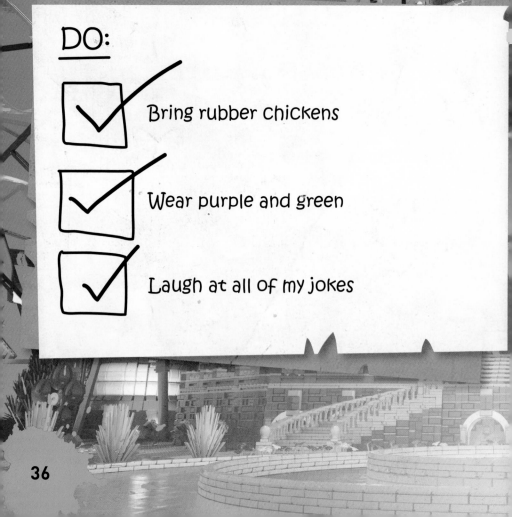

DO NOT:

 Wear black (or yellow)

 Wear long black capes and drive bat-like vehicles

 Wear black cowls with pointy ears

Gotham City's Villains

The Rogues aren't the only villains in Gotham City. There are many odd outlaws committing crimes. There are villains dressed as animals, like Zebra-Man, March Harriet and Orca.

The Mime

March Harriet

Orca

There are even villains who base their crimes on numbers, like The Calculator. All of these villains have one thing in common – they want to help the Joker defeat Batman!

Kite Man

The Eraser

Calendar Man

The Calculator

Zebra-Man

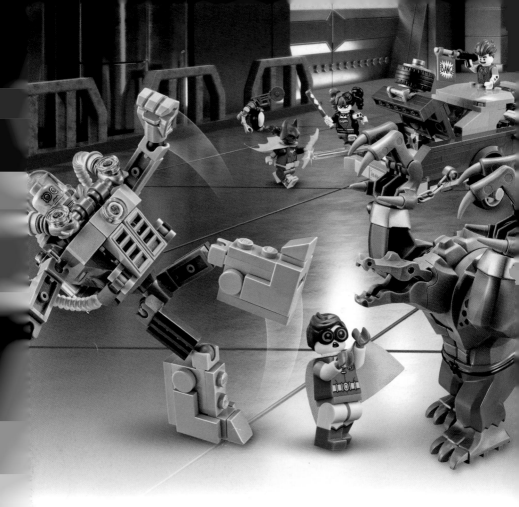

Villains vs. the Hero Team

The Joker and his allies attack
the Gotham City Energy Facility!
It will take great teamwork for the
Hero Team to defeat the villains.

Batman takes on Clayface and the Riddler. Robin tackles Mr. Freeze and Killer Croc. Batgirl battles with the Joker and Harley Quinn. The Hero Team must win!

Locked Up

Hurrah! Batman, Batgirl and Robin have put an end to the Joker's plan and defeated him.

All of the Rogues have been captured. They are now locked up in Arkham Asylum. Gotham City is safe once more. Thanks, Hero Team!

Quiz

1. Who is going to take over from Jim Gordon as Head of Police?

2. What kind of hat does the Penguin wear?

3. How does the police commissioner ask Batman for help?

4. How does Poison Ivy plan to trap Batman?

5. What kind of weapon does Harley Quinn use?

6. What is Catwoman's favourite thing to steal?

7. What does the Joker want to destroy?

8. Where are the Rogues now locked up?

Answers on page 48

Glossary

allies
A group of people who work together for a purpose.

Arkham Asylum
A hospital where Gotham's worst criminals
are locked away.

citizen
Someone who lives in a town or city.

crook
A person who is dishonest or a criminal.

fearsome
Very frightening.

foe
An enemy or opponent.

gang
An organised group
of criminals.

scientist
A person who studies science
and solves problems by doing
experiments.

Guide for Parents

This book is part of an exciting four-level reading series for children, developing the habit of reading widely for both pleasure and information. These chapter books have a compelling main narrative to suit your child's reading ability. Each book is designed to develop your child's reading skills, fluency, grammar awareness, and comprehension in order to build confidence and engagement when reading.

Ready for a *Level 2* book

YOUR CHILD SHOULD

- be using phonics, including consonant blends, such as bl, gl and sm, to read unfamiliar words; and common word endings, such as plurals, ing, ed and ly.
- be using the storyline, illustrations and the grammar of a sentence to check and correct his/her own reading.
- be pausing briefly at commas, and for longer at full stops; and altering his/her expression to respond to question, exclamation and speech marks.

A VALUABLE AND SHARED READING EXPERIENCE

For many children, reading requires much effort but adult participation can make this both fun and easier. So here are a few tips on how to use this book with your child.

TIP 1 Check out the contents together before your child begins:

- read the text about the book on the back cover.
- read through and discuss the contents page together to heighten your child's interest and expectation.
- make use of unfamiliar or difficult words on the page in a brief discussion.
- chat about the reading features used in the book, such as headings, captions, lists or charts.

TIP 2 Support your child as he/she reads the story pages:

- give the book to your child to read and turn the pages.
- where necessary, encourage your child to break a word into syllables, sound out each one and then flow the syllables together. Ask him/her to reread the sentence to check the meaning.
- when there's a question mark or an exclamation mark, encourage your child to vary his/her voice as he/she reads the sentence. Demonstrate how to do this if it is helpful.

TIP 3 Praise, share and chat:

- ask questions about the text and the meaning of the words used. These help to develop comprehension skills and awareness of the language used.

A FEW ADDITIONAL TIPS

- Try and read together every day. Little and often is best. These books are divided into manageable chapters for one reading session. However after 10 minutes, only keep going if your child wants to read on.
- Always encourage your child to have a go at reading difficult words by themselves. Praise any self-corrections, for example, "I like the way you sounded out that word and then changed the way you said it, to make sense."
- Read other books of different types to your child just for enjoyment and information.

Index

Answers to the quiz on pages 44:

1. Barbara Gordon 2. A top hat 3. With the Bat-Signal
4. With her tangling tendrils 5. A swinging bat 6. Precious gems
7. Gotham City Energy Facility 8. Arkham Asylum